How to Analyze the Works of

ANDREW
LLOYD WEBBER

by Katie Marsico

ABDO
Publishing Company

Essential Critiques

How to Analyze the Works of

ANDREW
LLOYD WEBBER

by Katie Marsico

Content Consultant: Shawn–Marie Garrett, DFA
Assistant professor of theatre
Barnard College, Columbia University

Credits

Published by ABDO Publishing Company, 8000 West 78th Street, Edina, Minnesota 55439. Copyright © 2011 by Abdo Consulting Group, Inc. International copyrights reserved in all countries. No part of this book may be reproduced in any form without written permission from the publisher. The Essential Library™ is a trademark and logo of ABDO Publishing Company.

Printed in the United States of America,
North Mankato, Minnesota
062010
092010

Editor: Amy Van Zee
Copy Editor: Jennifer Joline Anderson
Interior Design and Production: Marie Tupy
Cover Design: Marie Tupy

Library of Congress Cataloging-in-Publication Data
Marsico, Katie, 1980-
  How to analyze the works of Andrew Lloyd Webber / Katie Marsico.
     p. cm. — (Essential critiques)
  Includes bibliographical references and index.
  ISBN 978-1-61613-533-1
1. Lloyd Webber, Andrew, 1948—Criticism and interpretation—Juvenile literature. 2. Musicals—History and criticism—Juvenile literature. I. Title.
  ML3930.L58M37 2010
  782.1'4092—dc22
                                        2010015881

Table of Contents

1

Introduction to Critiques

What Is Critical Theory?

What do you usually do when you watch a musical theater production? You probably enjoy listening to the songs, viewing the set and the costumes, and watching the choreography. You learn about the characters as they are developed through dialogue and other interactions. You might be drawn in by the plot of the musical, eager to find out what happens at the end. Yet these are only a few of many possible ways of understanding and appreciating a musical. What if you are interested in delving more deeply? You might want to learn more about the composer and how his or her personal background is reflected in the production. Or you might want to examine what the production says about society—how it depicts the roles of women

and minorities, for example. If so, you have entered the realm of critical theory.

Critical theory helps you learn how various works of art, literature, music, theater, film, and other endeavors either support or challenge the way society behaves. Critical theory is the evaluation and interpretation of a work using different philosophies, or schools of thought. Critical theory can be used to understand all types of cultural productions.

There are many different critical theories. If you are analyzing a musical, each theory asks you to look at the work from a different perspective. Some theories address social issues, while others focus on the composer's life, what role the music plays in the overall production, or the time period in which the musical was written or set. For example, the critical theory that asks how a composer's life affected the work is called biographical criticism. Other common schools of criticism include historical criticism, feminist criticism, psychological criticism, and New Criticism, which examines a work solely within the context of the work itself.

What Is the Purpose of Critical Theory?

Critical theory can open your mind to new ways of thinking. It can help you evaluate a musical from a new perspective, directing your attention to issues and messages you may not otherwise recognize in a work. For example, applying feminist criticism to a theater production may make you aware of female stereotypes perpetuated in the work. Applying a critical theory to a work helps you learn about the person who created it or the society that enjoyed it. You can explore how the musical is perceived by current cultures.

How Do You Apply Critical Theory?

You conduct a critique when you use a critical theory to examine and question a work. The theory you choose is a lens through which you can view the work, or a springboard for asking questions about the work. Applying a critical theory helps you to think critically about the work. You are free to question the work and make an assertion about it. If you choose to examine a musical using biographical theory, for example, you want to know how the composer's personal background or education inspired or shaped the work. You could explore why the composer was drawn to the story. For instance, are there any parallels between a particular character's life and the composer's life?

Forming a Thesis

Ask your question and find answers in the work or other related materials. Then you can create a thesis. The thesis is the key point in your critique. It is your argument about the work based on the tenets, or beliefs, of the theory you are using. For example, if you are using biographical theory to ask how the composer's life inspired the work, your

How to Make
a Thesis Statement

In a critique, a thesis statement typically appears at the end of the introductory paragraph. It is usually only one sentence long and states the author's main idea.

How to Support
a Thesis Statement

A critique should include several arguments. Arguments support a thesis claim. An argument is one or two sentences long and is supported by evidence from the work being discussed.

Organize the arguments into paragraphs. These paragraphs make up the body of the critique.

thesis could be worded as follows: Composer Teng Xiong, raised in refugee camps in southeast Asia, drew upon her experiences to write the musical production *No Home for Me*.

Providing Evidence

Once you have formed a thesis, you must provide evidence to support it. Evidence might take the form of examples and quotations from the work itself—such as lyrics from a musical. Articles about the production or personal interviews with the composer might also support your ideas. You may wish to address what other critics have written about the work. Quotes from these individuals may help support your claim. If you find any quotes or examples that contradict your thesis, you will need to create an argument against them. For instance: Many critics have pointed to the heroine of *No Home for Me* as a powerless victim of circumstances. However, in the song "My Destiny," she is clearly depicted as someone who seeks to shape her own future.

In This Book

In this book, you will read overviews of famous musical productions by composer Andrew Lloyd Webber, each followed by a critique. Each critique will use one theory and apply it to one work. Critical thinking sections will give you a chance to consider other theses and questions about the work. Did you agree with the author's application of the theory? What other questions are raised by the thesis and its arguments? You can also find out what other critics think about each particular musical. Then, in the You Critique It section in the final pages of this book, you will have an opportunity to create your own critique.

Look for the Guides

Throughout the chapters that analyze the works, thesis statements have been highlighted. The box next to the thesis helps explain what questions are being raised about the work. Supporting arguments have been underlined. The boxes next to the arguments help explain how these points support the thesis. Look for these guides throughout each critique.

Andrew Lloyd Webber showed musical talent from a young age.

2

A Closer Look at Andrew Lloyd Webber

Andrew Lloyd Webber was born in London, England, on March 22, 1948. His mother, Jean Hermione Johnstone, was a piano teacher, and his father, William Lloyd Webber, served on the faculty of the Royal College of Music in London. Andrew and his younger brother, Julian, showed a fondness for music at an early age. The pair frequently staged brief productions for their family using a toy theater that their aunt, an actress, had encouraged them to build.

Music and Controversy

Lloyd Webber completed high school at London's Westminster School in 1965. He briefly studied history at Magdalen College, a school at Oxford University in Oxford, England. At about this time, he met lyricist Tim Rice, with whom he would collaborate on several musical projects. Eager to concentrate on composing, Lloyd Webber left Oxford in the winter of 1965, after only one term of study. In 1966, he and Rice created *The Likes of Us,* a show about children's homes in Great Britain in the late 1800s. It did not reach the stage, however, until 2005. In 1967, Lloyd Webber transferred to the Royal College of Music, where he began taking courses related to musical theater.

He continued to work with Rice. From 1967 to 1968, the pair busily crafted an early version of what would become *Joseph and the Amazing Technicolor Dreamcoat*—their acclaimed song-and-dance account of the biblical Joseph. By the time Lloyd Webber finished his classes at the Royal College, he had written nine musicals and was well on his way to fame. He and Rice debuted their first professional production, *Jesus Christ Superstar*, on Broadway in New York on October 12, 1971.

While *Superstar* won fame for Lloyd Webber, it also stirred controversy because of its portrayal of Christ in the context of a flamboyant rock opera. The show was condemned by some religious groups and banned in some parts of the world.

Tim Rice, *left*, and Andrew Lloyd Webber in 1973

Marriages and Fame

In 1971, Lloyd Webber married his first wife, Sarah Tudor Hugill. The couple had two children together. As Lloyd Webber's family grew, so did his career as a Broadway composer. *Evita*, the musical tale of former Argentinean First Lady Eva Perón, opened on June 21, 1978. The production was another Rice collaboration, and it soon won praise for both its score and lyrics.

After *Evita*, Rice and Lloyd Webber parted ways to explore new partnerships and creative projects. Lloyd Webber soon teamed up with director and lyricist Trevor Nunn to develop *Cats*, a musical adaptation of poet T. S. Eliot's *Old Possum's Book of Practical Cats*. The fantastical play, featuring cats as characters, debuted on May 11, 1981.

It was through *Cats* that Lloyd Webber met Sarah Brightman, one of the show's performers. Brightman would eventually become one of his most well-known leading ladies, both onstage and off. In 1983, Lloyd Webber divorced his first wife. He and Brightman wed in 1984.

That same year saw the premiere of his production *Starlight Express*. The rock musical features actors on roller skates. It was the composer's next musical, however, *The Phantom of the Opera*, that has perhaps earned him the greatest acclaim to date.

Opening on October 9, 1986, *Phantom* tells the hauntingly romantic story of a physically deformed, reclusive musician and his beautiful student in late nineteenth-century Paris, France. Lyricists Richard Stilgoe and Charles Hart collaborated with Lloyd Webber on what has since become the longest-running show on Broadway. Brightman was the first actress to take the role of the Phantom's love interest, Christine. The play was successful, but Brightman and Lloyd Webber's marriage ended in divorce in 1990.

Lloyd Webber continued his creative output. *Aspects of Love* debuted in 1989 and features lyrics by Hart and Don Black. *Sunset Boulevard*, Lloyd Webber's take on the 1950 film of the same name, followed in 1993 with lyrics by Black and Charles Hampton. Meanwhile, in 1991, Lloyd Webber married Madeleine Astrid Gurdon. By 2010, the couple had three children together.

New Collaborations

While few of his later productions have matched the popularity of *Superstar, Evita, Cats,* or *Phantom,* Lloyd Webber continues to create. Since the late 1990s, he has collaborated with respected lyricists such as Don Black, Jim Steinman, Alan Ayckbourn, Ben Elton, and David Zippel. *Whistle Down the Wind*, which premiered in 1996, is Lloyd

Webber's musical account of a group of children growing up in the rural South in the 1950s. That year also marked the debut of *By Jeeves*, Lloyd Webber's melodic look at the comic adventures of a British aristocrat and his faithful butler.

In 2000, audiences watched the curtain rise on *The Beautiful Game*, a tale of the lives and loves of members of an Irish football team. In 2002, Lloyd Webber produced A. R. Rahman's *Bombay Dreams*, a musical account of ambition, fame, and romance set against the backdrop of India's film industry. Lloyd Webber's adaptation of the Victorian ghost story *The Woman in White* debuted in 2004. Then, in March 2010, he made news headlines with the London premiere of *Love Never Dies*, the highly anticipated sequel to *Phantom*.

Lloyd Webber has been honored by England's Queen Elizabeth II, who knighted him in 1992 and declared him a British lord in 1997. He has also received numerous theater and music awards, including three Grammys and seven Tonys. Several of his musicals have been adapted into major motion pictures. His song "You Must Love Me" from the movie *Evita* earned both an Academy Award and a Golden Globe for Best Original Song.

Lloyd Webber oversees seven theaters he currently owns in London. He has been forced to address health issues as well, including prostate cancer. His diagnosis was revealed to the public in October 2009, and, after surgery, he announced he was cancer-free in 2010. Lloyd Webber continues his work, brainstorming with a multitude of lyricists, producers, performers, and stage crews, and adding to his musicals that writers have been critiquing for the past four decades.

In 2009, Lloyd Webber celebrated the nine-thousandth performance of *The Phantom of the Opera* at the Majestic Theatre in New York City.

Joanna Ampil and Steve Balsamo portrayed Mary Magdalene and Jesus Christ in a 1996 production of *Jesus Christ Superstar.*

3

An Overview of
Jesus Christ Superstar

Jesus Christ Superstar opened on Broadway on October 12, 1971. The rock opera retells a famous biblical story in an unconventional manner, incorporating modern musical styles, comically anachronistic slang, and flamboyant costumes and stage sets. Based upon the New Testament's Gospel according to John, the musical recounts the final week in the life of Jesus Christ.

As the story begins, Judas (an apostle of Jesus) laments that although he still loves and respects Jesus, he is disturbed by the fact that an increasing number of frenzied crowds are hailing him as the Messiah—Jesus is becoming a superstar. Judas worries the Jewish Pharisees (the religious leaders) and Roman authorities will view Jesus as a challenge to their own power.

Jesus, on the other hand, tries to calm his followers. He says none of them should worry about the future when all their fates ultimately lie in God's hands. When Jesus appears overwhelmed by his disciples' constant questioning, reformed prostitute Mary Magdalene tries to comfort and calm him by wiping his forehead and singing soothingly. Later in act 1, she performs one of the work's most famous songs—"I Don't Know How to Love Him"—in which she explains that Jesus is like no other man she has ever met.

Plans to Betray

The first act features scenes based on New Testament stories, including Jesus's procession into Jerusalem on Palm Sunday and his chastisement of the money changers in the temple there. It also reveals Judas's ongoing crisis of conscience. By the conclusion of act 1, Judas has agreed to tell religious leaders Caiaphas and Annas of Jesus's whereabouts so they can arrest him. The high priests plan to accuse Jesus of blasphemy because he has proclaimed himself to be the Messiah.

As the second act begins, the audience sees Jesus sitting down to the Last Supper, the famous final meal Christ shared with his apostles. During this gathering, he reveals that Judas will soon betray him. The tormented disciple angrily tries to explain himself but finally leaves in frustration. While Judas searches for authorities so they can proceed with the arrest, Jesus waits in anguish in the garden of Gethsemane. Realizing death is near, he expresses fear, resentment, and, ultimately, acceptance.

Judas returns to Jesus in the garden and kisses him on the cheek. Acting on this prearranged signal, guards swoop in and take Jesus into custody. As he is led to Caiaphas and Annas, Jesus is followed by a mob of news reporters. The crowd of reporters is just one example of how the production injects modern details into an ancient story, to ironic effect.

Crucifixion of Christ

As act 2 progresses, Jesus is paraded before the Pharisees, Pilate, and Herod, king of Judea. The religious leaders beg Pilate to crucify Jesus, as they have no law of their own to justify putting a man to death. King Herod challenges Jesus to "[c]hange my water into wine" and "[w]alk across my swimming pool."[1] Herod sulkily orders Jesus to return to

Pilate's court when he fails to perform the miracles on command. Meanwhile, Judas catches a glimpse of his former leader, who is by now exhausted after enduring interrogation from his many judges and mockery from the mobs and guards. Crippled with guilt, the disciple realizes he is simply one small part of God's master plan. He understands he cannot escape his fate, which he anticipates will be forever defined by his betrayal of Jesus. Overwhelmed by grief and hopelessness, Judas takes his own life.

Back at Pilate's palace, the crowds are crying for Jesus to be crucified. Yet the Roman governor hesitates to pass such a brutal sentence. Like Judas, he fears he will one day be blamed for condemning an innocent man to death. In an effort to appease the mob, he orders Jesus flogged 39 times, but the beating does little to satisfy their thirst for blood. After the last stroke of the lash, Pilate practically begs his prisoner to give him any possible reason to avoid sending him to the cross. Yet Jesus has already accepted what lies ahead as being God's will, and he does not defend himself.

An unsettled Pilate regretfully gives the crowd what they wish, and Jesus is crucified. Before he dies, Jesus hallucinates. He envisions Judas, echoed

by a choir, asking if he truly believes himself to be the Messiah and the Son of God.

After Jesus perishes on the cross, the musical concludes with his remaining apostles looking to one another for comfort and insight on how their lives have been changed. *Jesus Christ Superstar* as a whole addresses issues such as faith, human nature, and individuals' relationships with God.

Christopher Murray played the role of Jesus in a German production of *Jesus Christ Superstar* in 2005.

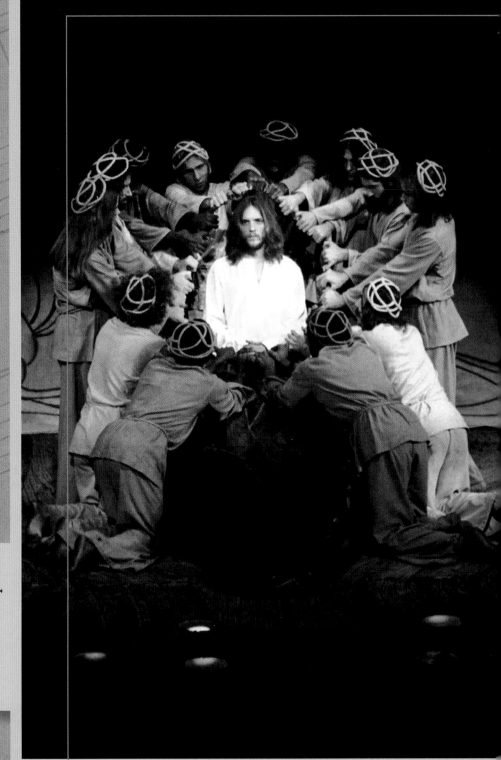

Jesus is surrounded by his 12 disciples.

4

How to Apply Historical Criticism to *Jesus Christ Superstar*

What Is Historical Criticism?

Critics applying historical criticism to a musical consider the historical context during which the work was created or produced. They ask how the production reflects the social, economic, and political realities of its time. First, critics need to research the era during which the composer wrote the piece. What important events or social changes occurred?

Next, critics identify the play's major themes, or main ideas. How do these connect to what was happening in the world at the time the production was being developed? How do characters' attitudes and actions or other plot events reflect the historical period?

Critiquing *Jesus Christ Superstar*

When *Jesus Christ Superstar* was first staged in the early 1970s, North America and Europe were experiencing rapid social change. It was a period commonly referred to as the "flower power era." Young people led the times. As they protested the war in Vietnam, they also questioned mainstream ideals in fashion, music, politics, morals, and faith, stressing individual thought as opposed to conformity. Lloyd Webber's *Superstar* is a product of its time, reflecting the individualism and open-mindedness about faith, spirituality, and religion that was typical of the youth culture of the 1960s and 1970s.

Evidence of this can be found in the unconventional characterization of biblical heroes and antiheroes. In traditional religious plays, films, and art, biblical prophets and apostles as well as Jesus himself are often portrayed reverently. Yet Lloyd Webber's

---

Thesis Statement

The thesis statement in this critique is "Lloyd Webber's *Superstar* is a product of its time, reflecting the individualism and open-mindedness about faith, spirituality, and religion that was typical of the youth culture of the 1960s and 1970s." The thesis addresses the following question: In what ways does *Superstar* reflect the era in which it was created? This argument emphasizes the growing belief in the importance of experience, spirituality, and self-discovery during the 1960s and 1970s.

characters are complex, multidimensional figures with all the flaws of ordinary human beings. They are shown questioning God's will and drawing their own conclusions based on personal experience. The play's characterization of biblical figures reflects the liberal attitudes of the 1960s and 1970s, a time when people evaluated scripture as it related to ordinary experience rather than abstract morality.

The characters in *Superstar* experience a range of feelings and attitudes as they attempt to understand their existence and religion. Even Jesus is not without fault. He becomes impatient with his disciples and the countless people who beg him to perform miracles. In "Gethsemane," he bitterly questions the mission God has set him on, which he knows will end with the cross. "Can you show me now that I would not be killed in vain?" he asks while sitting in the garden of Gethsemane the night before his crucifixion. "Show me just a little of your omnipresent brain / Show me there's a reason for your wanting me to die."[1] Within the same song, however, Jesus renews his faith and accepts that he will do his heavenly Father's bidding. "God thy will is hard," he declares. "But you hold every card."[2] Lloyd Webber's portrayal of Jesus shows him

Argument One

The author is giving an example of a character who reflects the youth culture of the 1960s and 1970s. She shows how the musical's creators chose to give Jesus doubts about God's master plan: "Lloyd Webber's portrayal of Jesus shows him feeling doubt and questioning his purpose. Such profound doubts about accepted truths were common themes in works of popular culture in the 1960s and 1970s."

feeling doubt and questioning his purpose. Such profound doubts about accepted truths were common themes in works of popular culture in the 1960s and 1970s.

Jesus is not the only one to demonstrate doubt or to struggle with God and religion. Few of the roles in *Superstar* can be categorized in the simple, black-or-white manner that traditionally defines villains and heroes.

Judas is one of the musical's most important characters. He betrays Jesus, but he has his own motives for turning his teacher over to the Pharisees. Judas is unsure whether Jesus truly is the Messiah. He also worries that Jesus's superstar status is endangering his followers and overshadowing what he perceives to be more meaningful purposes to their mission, including helping the poor. By the time Judas prepares to commit suicide in the second act, though, he has managed to better comprehend his own relationship with and belief in a higher power. And, while his

faith is unique because it is shaped by anger, it is a form of faith all the same.

William Byrne portrayed Jesus in a German production of *Jesus Christ Superstar.*

Judas blames God for having slotted him to go down in history as the traitor who led to Jesus's downfall. From Judas's perspective, his actions — as well as everyone else's — are part of a divine master plan. However, he does not simply accept God's will; he questions it: "God I'll never ever know," he laments, "why you chose me for your crime."[3] As is the case with Jesus, Pontius Pilate, Mary

Magdalene, and other characters in *Superstar*, his faith is based on individual experiences and independent thought. <u>Like the younger generation that ushered in the flower power era of the 1960s and 1970s, Judas questions authority rather than blindly accepting it.</u>

<u>Not only do character and plot development reflect a new approach to humans' relationship with God. So does the music.</u> In contrast to traditional masses, hymns, and orchestral pieces composed for religious services, Lloyd Webber's music is catchy and poppy, with witty, slang-filled lyrics. To some, it may seem better suited to a heavy metal concert than to a theatrical production about the life of Christ. In fact, some audiences considered Lloyd Webber's work to be sacrilegious because his

---

Argument Two

The author is giving another example of a character who reflects the youth culture of the 1960s and 1970s. She discusses the portrayal of Judas as a character of the times: "Like the younger generation that ushered in the flower power era of the 1960s and 1970s, Judas questions authority rather than blindly accepting it."

Argument Three

The author has now turned to the second element of her thesis. Her previous points discussed characters, but she now argues how the music is a reflection of the youth culture of the 1960s and 1970s: "Not only do character and plot development reflect a new approach to humans' relationship with God. So does the music." She emphasizes how new types of music such as rock and roll are used to tell these traditional stories.

use of rock and roll and other pop elements did not seem properly reverent. Yet Lloyd Webber's score is compelling for its day. It contemporizes the tension and inner conflict that biblical figures—and modern audiences—experience as they struggle with their faith.

Lloyd Webber, who was in his early twenties when he began working on *Superstar*, was part of a younger generation that was influenced by the

Through music, costumes, and character development, Jesus Christ Superstar reflects the era in which it was created.

Conclusion

This final paragraph is the conclusion of the critique. It summarizes the author's arguments, which have been supported with evidence from *Superstar*. The author also discusses Lloyd Webber's age during the time he wrote these musicals, and how he himself was influenced by what was happening around him. This is typical of historical criticism, in which the critic analyzes how the society, economy, and political system of the era are reflected in a work of literature and art.

changing times. Not everyone was initially enthusiastic about his treatment of religious topics, but the musical does not aim for a tried-and-true formula that pleases traditionally conservative churchgoing audiences. Instead, like the era in which it was created, the musical reflects the belief that different people can have different approaches toward faith and God that allow for individual expression and independent thought.

Thinking Critically about *Jesus Christ Superstar*

Now it's your turn to assess the critique. Consider these questions:

1. The thesis statement asserts that *Superstar* was a product of its time. The author cites examples of characters and musical styles from the production to support her claim. What other elements of the musical might have been considered to support the thesis?

2. Can you think of any characters or plot elements that would serve as evidence against the author's thesis?

3. Which argument in the critique do you think is the strongest? Which was the most interesting? Can you think of any more characters from the musical whose actions would support the thesis?

Other Approaches

What you have just read is one way to apply historical criticism to *Jesus Christ Superstar*. Other writers have approached the musical in different ways. Historical criticism takes into account what was happening during the time in which the piece was written. Following are two alternate approaches to the musical.

Superstar as a Reflection of Anti-Semitism

In the 1960s and 1970s, race and religion were hot topics in U.S. culture. White supremacist groups preached a hatred for Jewish people. When *Superstar* premiered on the stage, some individuals who critiqued the production believed it was influenced by discrimination against members of the Jewish faith, because it is the Jews in the play who push for Jesus to be crucified. Well-known human rights activist Marc H. Tanenbaum made several public statements to this effect in the early 1970s. "The authors," he argues, "have written a scenario in which there are heroes and villains, and the Jews are the villains."[4]

The thesis statement for a related critique might assert: The portrayal of Jewish leaders as the villains of *Jesus Christ Superstar* is a reflection of anti-Semitism.

Superstar and Hippie Ideology

The hippie movement emerged in the United States and some parts of Europe in the 1960s and 1970s. Hippies were generally young people rebelling against the norms of mainstream culture. They emphasized love and peace. Many wore brightly colored clothing and unconventionally long hairstyles to symbolize their freedom from the older generations' conservative values. Writer Martin Brady reviewed a 2009 production of *Superstar* and called it "the ultimate hippie passion." He wrote that it "exuded sincerity and entertainingly exploited its memorable score and message of love and sacrifice."[5]

A thesis statement for a critique that considers hippie culture might be: In *Jesus Christ Superstar*, pop music and general enthusiasm convey a younger generation's emphasis on love.

Evita was staged on Broadway for the first time in 1979.

5

An Overview of *Evita*

Andrew Lloyd Webber's *Evita* opened on June 21, 1978, in London. The musical, which recounts the story of famous Argentinean First Lady Eva Perón, premiered on Broadway a little more than a year later. *Evita* won numerous Tony Awards and was made into a film starring Madonna and Antonio Banderas in 1996.

The curtain opens on a scene set in the summer of 1952. Argentineans gathered in a movie theater lament the news of Eva's death. Everyone is distraught upon hearing of their beloved First Lady's downfall—all except for a student named Che, who serves mostly as the narrator throughout the remainder of the musical. "Che" is Che Guevara, the future guerrilla leader and Marxist revolutionary who opposed dictators in real life.

Che makes it clear to the audience that, unlike the masses that surround him, he sees Eva for who she really is: a self-interested ruler who may have been adored by the crowds but who in reality "did nothing for years."[1]

Humble Beginnings

The action then flashes back to show Eva in 1934. She is a young girl in a somewhat distasteful nightclub in rural Argentina. Eva begs a touring singer to take her to Buenos Aires, the nation's colorful and exciting capital city. The performer, Agustín Magaldi, reluctantly agrees. He soon learns, however, that he is just one of many men she will use to advance her career. For Eva, love affairs are a way to gain power in a male-dominated world. Once in Buenos Aires, she charms numerous men into granting her greater opportunities as an actress.

Almost a decade after her arrival there, Eva crosses paths with Colonel Juan Perón, a prominent military leader. Through Che's narration and songs such as "The Art of the Possible," audiences learn Argentina is in the midst of a politically unstable era when government heads rise quickly and fall just as suddenly as a result of luck, skill, and popularity.

Che serves mostly as the narrator in *Evita*.

Perón is on the rise, and Eva wastes no time in convincing him she is the right woman to be by his side. Eva tells Perón's mistress that he is through with her.

Yet, while she succeeds in wooing Perón and winning support among the common people, Eva fails to impress the nation's military establishment and wealthy aristocracy. These powerful groups resent her growing influence in government affairs. They have little regard for her lowly background or the fact that she has established herself simply by sharing the colonel's bed. By the conclusion of act 1, though, she has managed to help her future husband win the highest office in the country. Eva convinces the working class that he is a leader who will focus on their interests.

First Lady

As the curtain rises on the second act, Eva and President Perón address a crowd of supporters outside their palace. Eva delivers one of her most memorable musical numbers in the production— "Don't Cry for Me, Argentina." Che continues to narrate as the First Lady travels to Europe on a goodwill tour.

Upon Eva's return, she pledges to concentrate more on the needs of her own people by promoting charities to benefit the underprivileged. She also continues her battle against members of the aristocracy, who oppress Argentina's poor and continue to look down upon her personally. Yet, while the nation's humble workers worship her as a saint, Che is less enthusiastic. He sometimes directly addresses Eva and at other moments offers musical commentary to the audience. During "Waltz for Eva and Che," he asks how Eva can claim she is a savior while ruthlessly persecuting her opposition.

Eva Perón lived from 1919 to 1952.

Failing Health

It grows more apparent toward the end of act 2 that Eva's health is rapidly declining. Though her ailment—cervical cancer—is never mentioned by name, the audience learns she is dying. Eva admits she is frustrated by "her own weak body" but fights for more power in spite of it.[2] She dreams of becoming vice president, though her opponents rally against her, and she ultimately proves too sick to overcome them.

As she reaches the end of her life, she reflects on the dazzling and memorable moments that have filled her short time on Earth. Eva considers the choices she has made. Had she not fought so hard to see her ambitions fulfilled, she might have been healthier and known the joys of a humbler, quieter existence as an average Argentinean wife and mother. But then Eva might never have reached the status of a national idol who earned the love of Perón and the people. When she at last perishes, her supporters are shaken and devastated by the loss. A brief but chilling epilogue recited by Che reveals how a monument was planned for the permanent display of her body, but its construction was never completed. In the wake of a military coup, her body disappeared for nearly 17 years.

Professional theater critics and audiences alike have applauded Lloyd Webber's production for its musical score. Certain numbers are bold and

fast moving, while others are quieter and elegantly poetic. Combined with Tim Rice's lyrics, they tell the tale of an unforgettable heroine driven by an appetite for power and fame.

Madonna won a Golden Globe for her performance in the 1996 film version of *Evita*.

Evita has received praise from critics for its score and choreography.

6

How to Apply Feminist Criticism to *Evita*

What Is Feminist Criticism?

People who apply feminist criticism—sometimes referred to as gender criticism—to a musical analyze how masculinity and femininity are represented onstage. They evaluate whether common gender stereotypes are perpetuated by the work.

Critics examine how female characters are depicted through their words, actions, and relationships with other characters. They note how women are viewed and treated within the context of the play. They try to determine what a performance says about females and their identities.

Critiquing *Evita*

Evita is the story of one influential woman and the impact she had on her nation and the people around her. Eva Perón is the main character; few other females besides chorus members and Juan Perón's displaced mistress share the spotlight with her. In addition, the female roles that are present are limited. The work's two leading females fall into classic stereotypes: the aggressively power-hungry, manipulative man-eater—Eva—and the helpless, easily conquered victim, represented by Perón's rejected mistress.

Tim Rice's lyrics make it apparent that Eva is ruled by her own steely determination to move forward. From the time she is introduced as a young girl in a run-down nightclub in rural Argentina, Eva is shown to be desperate for a better lot in life.

Thesis Statement

The thesis of this critique is "The work's two leading females fall into classic stereotypes: the aggressively power-hungry, manipulative man-eater— Eva—and the helpless, easily conquered victim, represented by Perón's rejected mistress." This particular thesis answers the following question: How are women depicted in *Evita*?

Argument One

The author presents arguments to support her thesis. This is her first argument: "Tim Rice's lyrics make it apparent that Eva is ruled by her own steely determination to move forward." This point addresses the first of the two gender stereotypes the author identifies in *Evita*.

She is aware that Argentinean society is shaped by men, who dominate everything from business to government. When Eva begs singer Agustín Magaldi to take her to Buenos Aires, Argentina, at the beginning of the play, he cautions her by saying, "Eva, beware your ambition / It's hungry and cold / can't be controlled / will run wild."[1]

Just as Eva convinces Magaldi to bring her to Buenos Aires, she persuades Colonel Juan Perón to pursue political power so "we" can seize the highest office in the country. "All you have to do is sit and wait," Eva coos to him toward the end of act 1. "Keeping out of everybody's way / We'll . . . *you'll* be handed power on a plate."[2] Eva's slip of the tongue is significant, as it helps the audience see that Eva wants power not only for her husband's sake but for herself. Yet she also understands that she must tread a careful path while pursuing her ambitions. Eva grasps that her society will not readily accept a woman as a national leader. Eva is a skilled manipulator who enjoys a career as an actress and who knows how to play many different parts in real life, too. In order to win control over those around her, she can slip into the role of a supportive wife, champion of the underclass, or international ambassador.

As narrator, Che never hesitates to remind everyone that, while some Argentineans perceive the First Lady as a saint, he sees her for what she really is and for what the writers have designed the heroine to be—a fiercely ambitious woman capable of manipulating powerful men. Che's words even hint that Eva might be guilty of political crimes. He calls out Eva's hypocrisy during "Waltz for Eva and Che": "How can you claim you're our savior / When those who oppose you are stepped on / Or cut up, or simply disappear?"[3]

In addition to her political ambition, the lyrics and the plot imply that Eva uses numerous men as stepping-stones in furthering her career and fame. Her relationships with Magaldi, Perón, and others do not seem to be fueled so much by affection as ambition. Her love affairs are chances to acquaint herself with male characters who can be of benefit to her. One early scene shows Eva lying on a mattress on

> **Argument Two**
> The author provides a second example of Eva as being hungry for power: "In addition to her political ambition, the lyrics and the plot imply that Eva uses numerous men as stepping-stones in furthering her career and fame."

one side of a revolving door. One by one, men visit her. Each one is better dressed than the last. And after each one leaves, Eva herself becomes better dressed, too. The scene is a depiction of her use of men as stepping-stones.

Patti LuPone starred as Eva Perón when *Evita* ran on Broadway in 1979.

If Eva represents the rapacious, power-hungry man-eater, Perón's young mistress represents another feminine stereotype: the helpless victim. The young woman is meek, submissive, and quickly overthrown by her more aggressive successor. She has nothing to say when Eva emphatically tells her that her romance with the colonel is over and that she must leave his home.

The girl does not even have a formal name in the musical; she is simply "Perón's mistress." She is depicted as pitiable and pathetic—someone who deserves little recognition, feels sorry for herself, and accepts that only sorrow and failure will fill her life. "I don't expect my love affairs to last for long," she laments in "Another Suitcase in Another Hall." "Never fool myself that my dreams will come true / Being used to trouble I anticipate it / But all the same I hate it, wouldn't you?"[4]

Perón's mistress is the opposite of Eva. And as one of two notable female characters in the play, she

reflects one of two basic roles for women in Lloyd Webber's production.

A scene from a 2006 London production of *Evita*

With no clear ambitions of her own, Perón's mistress is used by a man and appears prepared to endure endless misery. Eva, on the other hand, does not seem to make a move that is not motivated by ambition. She uses men and continues to grasp for authority until her health starts to fail. The helpless, easily conquered weakling and the power-hungry, controlling political climber are the primary female forces in Lloyd Webber's *Evita*. The play does not feature a woman who falls into any true

Conclusion

This final paragraph is the conclusion of the critique. The author restates her thesis and reminds the readers that the women in the musical are depicted in one of two ways. The author also discusses how these depictions reinforce gender stereotypes.

middle ground. As such, the play reinforces stereotypes that women cannot define their own destinies, set goals, or achieve happiness without manipulating men and, in the case of Eva, society as a whole.

Thinking Critically about *Evita*

Now it's your turn to assess the critique. Consider these questions:

1. The essay critiques *Evita* through the lens of feminist criticism, examining how women are depicted in the musical. Can you think of additional questions or issues a critic might raise in a feminist analysis of *Evita*?

2. The author has supported her points by examining characterization and plot. Can you think of any other elements of the production, such as musical style or costumes, that could be examined to find support for the thesis?

3. The author concludes that *Evita* reinforces the stereotypical view of women as unable to define their own destinies, set goals, or achieve happiness without resorting to manipulation. Does the musical reinforce any other stereotypes about women, or any about men?

Other Approaches

The essay you have just read is one way to apply feminist criticism to *Evita*. Following are two additional approaches using feminist criticism.

The Tango and the Femme Fatale Role

In a 1997 article featured in the journal *Latin American Perspectives*, dance theorist and historian Marta E. Savigliano discusses how a famous Latin American dance called the tango is used in the film version of *Evita* to shape certain gender stereotypes surrounding the character of Eva. Savigliano argues that the choreography is one way in which the production identifies the heroine as a femme fatale, or a beautiful temptress who knows how to manipulate and control men. Savigliano explains, "Producing these tangoesque images of Evita . . . projects a universal image of a femme fatale . . . that makes femmes fatales fascinating in their difference and yet recognizable or easy to identify with as generic women with power."[5]

The thesis statement for a critique discussing the role of the tango might be: By using the tango as an artistic element in the musical, Lloyd Webber adds to Eva's image as the stereotypical femme fatale— the charming, seductive, but dangerous woman who often brings about her own death or the deaths of those around her.

Analyzing Gender Opportunities

Writers who use feminist criticism often ask questions such as "Do female characters seem to have the same opportunities as male characters?" In a 2001 review of *Evita* in the *Honolulu Star-Bulletin,* journalist John Berger describes the play as "the story of an intelligent and ruthless woman who became the fifteen-year-old mistress of a popular singer, dumped the singer when she met a man better placed to advance her career, and repeated the process until she met Perón."[6] A critic could explore the storyline to see why Eva used romantic relationships to achieve success.

The thesis statement for such a critique might be: In *Evita*, ambitious women do not have the same opportunities as men. Instead, they must make their own opportunities and often resort to romantic involvement to do so.

Over the years, *Cats* has toured in more than 20 countries, including Argentina and Finland.

7

An Overview of *Cats*

When Lloyd Webber's *Cats* premiered in London
on May 11, 1981, the audience found themselves
immersed in a fantastical musical adventure about
a tribe of felines known as the Jellicles. Based on
famous poet T. S. Eliot's *Old Possum's Book of
Practical Cats*, the production has earned numerous
awards, including seven Tonys. *Cats* has become
one of the most popular musicals of all time thanks
to a combination of creative elements such as
elaborate makeup and costumes, witty lyrics, a
varied musical score, and intriguing characters.

Part of what makes the musical so appealing are
the whimsical, larger-than-life characters that Lloyd
Webber brings to the stage. As in Eliot's poems,
the cats have human personalities. They gather in a

junkyard one night of the year to celebrate their ties to the Jellicle clan and to select one member of their family who will make a mystical journey to what is referred to as the Heaviside Layer. Upon reaching this heavenlike destination, the chosen Jellicle will be reborn into a new life, in keeping with the timeless saying that cats have nine lives.

The felines share this information directly with the audience not long after the curtain rises in act 1. Though the Jellicles are initially mistrustful of the audience—much in the same way that real cats often behave—they eventually introduce themselves. The music shifts in tone as the main characters reveal their individual pasts and personalities. Each wants to demonstrate why he or she is the best candidate for a chance at rebirth. The production's extremely detailed makeup artistry and varied musical styles help each character stand out from the other cats that hope to be reborn.

Meeting the Cats

Jennyanydots is a large tabby famous for her lazy lounging; Rum Tum Tugger is a self-centered and hard-to-please tomcat. As patriarch of the clan, Old Deuteronomy is wise and well respected—he is the character who will ultimately decide which feline wins rebirth. Lloyd Webber presents several other intriguing Jellicles during act 1, including Grizabella, the Glamour Cat. She left the clan in her younger days to explore the world but now returns stumbling onto the stage, old and broken down. Her fellow felines mock Grizabella's withered appearance and shun her for her former lack of loyalty to the clan.

The other cats' cold response to Grizabella is just one example of the human characteristics and behaviors that Lloyd Webber's cats exhibit. They demonstrate disapproval and cruelty as well as support and compassion. They explain their actions and emotions. For instance, the Jellicles repeatedly sing about their fear of feline villain Macavity, who does not make his entrance until act 2.

The Villain Macavity

The first act concludes with a song-and-dance extravaganza known as the Jellicle Ball. The festivities are one of the traditions associated with the group's annual junkyard gathering. Grizabella seizes the celebration as an opportunity to reconnect with her family, but they again reject her.

Audiences finally receive a firsthand glimpse of the terrifying Macavity. This feared and hated enemy of the clan kidnaps Old Deuteronomy and then tries to return to the junkyard disguised as the patriarch. Several of the male Jellicles recognize his trickery, though, and they fight him until he retreats. Before Macavity departs, however, he causes an explosion that blackens the stage. Left in darkness, the cats are still without their beloved leader.

Luckily, however, the Jellicles have the Magical Mr. Mistoffelees, a sorcerer cat, on their side. Mr. Mistoffelees uses his magic to relight the junkyard and restore Old Deuteronomy to his family.

Rebirth

With the Jellicle leader returned, it is time to choose which feline will be sent to the Heaviside Layer and experience rebirth. In one of the most famous musical numbers, "Memory," Grizabella makes her case for why she should be selected. The faded Jellicle acknowledges that she has seen better days, and her recollections are now her only source of happiness. Yet she understands that winning reacceptance from the clan and being reborn would mean a return to the joy she once knew.

"I must wait for the sunrise," Grizabella declares. "I must think of a new life / And I mustn't give in / When the dawn comes / Tonight will be a memory too / And a new day will begin."[1] Her striking reflections move the other cats and convince them she should be the chosen one. After climbing aboard a large tire that rises toward the heavens, Grizabella leaves the junkyard alongside Old Deuteronomy but completes the last part of her journey on her own. Afterward, the cats each return home.

Betty Buckley performed as Grizabella in 1983.

Each of the main cats in the production has a unique appearance.

How to Apply New Criticism to *Cats*

What Is New Criticism?

New Criticism studies how all the various elements in a work come together to support a larger theme. New Criticism's entire focus is on the work itself. No attention is given to the creator's personal life or to the work's historical or cultural contexts.

Elements for analysis include lighting, sound effects, scenery, music, makeup, and lyrics, as well as characterization and plot. A person using New Criticism might ask, "How do these different parts of the musical work in unity to express a broader theme?" or "What multiple themes or meanings can be derived from the play?"

Critiquing *Cats*

Lloyd Webber's *Cats* portrays a fantastic world of personified felines that appeals to people of all ages. This tribe of cats displays anger, longing, sadness, and fear. The elements that make up the production—including costumes, lyrics, and music—combine to create a metaphor for human society and identity.

The use of makeup and costumes plays a particularly important role in emphasizing this broader theme that cats are like people in their variety and uniqueness. The characters' painted faces, wigs, leotards, and bodysuits reflect an astonishing variety of spots, stripes, fur, tails, and whiskers. This artistry reinforces the idea that cats, like people, have distinct appearances and personalities. For instance, Grizabella's scraggly eyebrows, grayish white face, and numerous

---

Thesis Statement

The thesis statement in this critique is as follows: "The elements that make up the production—including costumes, lyrics, and music—combine to create a metaphor for human society and identity." This thesis answers the following question: How do the various theatrical elements of the production *Cats* work together to support the musical's broader theme?

Argument One

The author has started to argue her thesis. The author begins her New Critical approach by analyzing costumes and makeup. This is her first point: "This artistry reinforces the idea that cats, like people, have distinct appearances and personalities."

Cats takes place in a junkyard.

wrinkles depict a feline of advanced age who has seen better days.

Rum Tum Tugger, on the other hand, sports bold brown, white, and black stripes. The female cats regard him as dashing and attractive, and his multiple colors hint at his complexity. Other characters may look at him and see a cat that is pleasing to the eye, but he himself is not easily pleased.

Combined with makeup and costumes the production's

> **Argument Two**
>
> The author has discussed how costumes and makeup support the themes outlined in the thesis. Her second point addresses lyrics: "Combined with makeup and costumes the production's lyrics help extend the allegory that cats exist in a society that functions like human society."

lyrics help extend the allegory that cats exist in
a society that functions like human society. As
Old Deuteronomy informs listeners in "The Ad-
Dressing of Cats," "You should need no interpreter
to understand our character / You've learned enough
to take the view / That cats are very much like
me and you."[1] Old Deuteronomy reveals that his
identity is both human- and catlike. He functions as
the tribe's leader. In the musical number "Prologue:
Jellicle Songs," the chorus lists the countless traits
and personality types that can be found within the
clan. Each cat has a distinct personality, and the

lyrics hint that the cats have jobs or specific beliefs. "Practical cats, dramatical cats / Pragmatical cats, fanatical cats . . . / Political cats, hypocritical cats / Clerical cats, hysterical cats" are some of the various types of cats that are listed during the song.[2]

The musical score does a great deal to support the theme, as well. Lloyd Webber treats audiences to a broad range of musical styles that reflect the characters' unique personalities and roles in their feline community. Classical, pop, jazz, and rock are all used to further define each of the felines. For instance, Old Deuteronomy is the trusted leader of the Jellicles—a patriarch who commands respect and whose Biblical name suggests his priestly role. It is therefore fitting that his "Ad-Dressing of Cats" at the end of the show sounds like a hymn. On the other hand, the ballad "Memory" is nostalgic but optimistic, much like the aging Grizabella who sings it in hopes of being chosen to travel to the Heaviside Layer.

Argument Three

Finally, the author discusses musical styles as the final element of the play that supports the themes outlined in the thesis. Her third point is as follows: "Lloyd Webber treats audiences to a broad range of musical styles that reflect the characters' unique personalities and roles in their feline community."

The creators use musical techniques to produce specific emotions in audience members. For example, minor chords are used to match portions of melancholy lyrics in "Memory." This has the potential to provoke an emotional response in the audience members. They may be more willing to suspend disbelief and believe more deeply in a world where cats live in a society like theirs. The varied choreography that accompanies the score achieves the same goal and features jazz moves, acrobatic maneuvers, ballet, and tap.

Some critics argue that there is no real plot in *Cats,* only a collection of various songs and dances. To some extent, this is true. Lloyd Webber's production is not so much about a complicated storyline as it is about a world that casts felines and human beings in a similar light. Each element of the play, including makeup, scenery, lyrics, music, and choreography, invites audiences to consider this idea and to indulge in the fantasy that is *Cats.*

Conclusion
This final paragraph is the conclusion of the critique. The author reiterates the points she made to support her thesis and addresses a common criticism made about *Cats.*

Thinking Critically about *Cats*

Now it's your turn to assess the critique. Consider these questions:

1. Can you think of additional ways someone using New Criticism to analyze the play might respond? What questions could he or she ask?

2. Now that you have reviewed the proof supporting the thesis statement, do you agree with the writer's thesis? Why or why not? What about the author's argument did you find the most convincing?

3. In her conclusion, the author addresses some criticisms about the lack of plot in *Cats*. Do you agree with the criticisms? Do you agree with her arguments against the criticisms?

Other Approaches

What you have just read is one way to apply New Criticism to *Cats*. What are some other ways writers have approached it? New Criticism takes into account the elements of the production itself to evaluate the themes of a work. Following are two alternate approaches.

Redemption and Rebirth

The themes of redemption and rebirth run throughout the plotline of *Cats*. The Jellicles gather each year to decide which cat will go to the Heaviside Layer to experience rebirth. One particular character, Grizabella, is herself redeemed by being forgiven and folded back into the Jellicle clan after having left at a young age. Reviewer Christine Kennedy writes, "Through the meandering stories and character studies, and amid the bursts of jollity there runs an undercurrent of nostalgia and meditations on mortality and salvation."[3]

The thesis for an essay that focuses on the theme of redemption might be as follows: Through lyrics, plotlines, and musical styles, Lloyd Webber's *Cats* solemnly focuses on the themes of mortality, forgiveness, and rebirth.

Plot versus Experience

Most critics of *Cats* acknowledge that the play features a multitude of theatrical elements that are stunning to the eyes and ears. Yet many individuals are skeptical of the musical, claiming the story lacks plot and is therefore unsuccessful as a thought-provoking piece of art. A writer could refute this claim by asserting the fantasy itself is the goal of the musical. As *Time* magazine's T. E. Kalem writes, "It is a triumph of motion over emotion. . . . One could say at the end of the evening . . . 'We had the experience but missed the meaning.' In *Cats*, the spectacle is the substance."[4]

A thesis for such an essay might be: Through fantastical stories, detailed makeup and costumes, and dramatic music, Lloyd Webber's production emphasizes experience over plot.

CAMERON MACKINTOSH and
THE REALLY USEFUL THEATRE COMPANY INC.
present

The
PHANTOM
of the
OPERA

Music by
ANDREW LLOYD WEBBER
Lyrics by **CHARLES HART**

Additional lyrics by **RICHARD STILGOE**
Book by **RICHARD STILGOE & ANDREW LLOYD WEBBER**
Inspired by the novel by **GASTON LEROUX**

Production design by **MARIA BJÖRNSON**   Lighting by **ANDREW BRIDGE**
Sound by **MARTIN LEVAN**   Musical Supervision & Direction **DAVID CADDICK**
Orchestrations by **DAVID CULLEN & ANDREW LLOYD WEBBER**

Musical Staging & Choreography by **GILLIAN LYNNE**

Directed by **HAROLD PRINCE**

The Phantom of the Opera is perhaps Lloyd Webber's best-known musical.

An Overview of
The Phantom of the Opera

Lloyd Webber's *The Phantom of the Opera* is
based on a novel by French author Gaston Leroux.
The production first opened in London on
October 9, 1986, and has since earned numerous
theater awards, including seven Tonys. In 2004,
director Joel Schumacher released a film version of
Lloyd Webber's *Phantom,* starring Gerard Butler
and Emmy Rossum.

The Paris Opera House

The year is 1905, and the scene is Paris. Aged
French aristocrat Viscount Raoul de Chagny is
attending an auction of various items that once
graced the Paris Opera House. One of the pieces
up for sale is a dazzling glass chandelier, which the
auctioneer hints played a role in a long-ago disaster.

As his assistants lift a sheet to unveil the massive light fixture, it is abruptly lit and raised amidst dramatic organ music.

With the chandelier in place, the scene shifts to the Paris Opera House decades earlier. The cast of the production *Hannibal* is rehearsing as the facility's new managers, Monsieurs Firmin and André, observe from the wings. The rehearsal is soon interrupted, however, when a backdrop crashes onstage, nearly injuring an ill-tempered diva named Carlotta and her male costar, Piangi. Members of the chorus nervously whisper to each other that the accident must have been the work of the Phantom of the Opera.

When an unsettled Carlotta storms offstage, refusing to continue with the show, Firmin and André panic about who will take her place. Meg Giry, the daughter of the dance mistress Madame Giry, insists beautiful chorus girl Christine Daaé is up to the challenge. The managers are initially skeptical but are quickly reassured as she begins singing. In the scene that follows, Christine delivers a stunning performance that wins over the crowds on opening night.

Gerard Butler starred as the Phantom in Joel Schumacher's 2004 film version of *The Phantom of the Opera.*

The Secret Tutor

After her successful performance, Christine is visited in her dressing room by the handsome young Raoul, the opera house's patron. Raoul recognizes Christine as a childhood sweetheart. Though they have been parted for years, both he and Christine still clearly share a deep affection. Yet Raoul is not her only admirer. Christine confesses that she has a mysterious vocal instructor who keeps watch over her. She has never actually seen her ghostly instructor, but she hears his voice and senses his presence. She believes this "angel of music" must have been sent by her dead father to guide her.[1] Actually, the tutor is the Phantom himself, a musical genius with a disfigured face, who lives in a secret room beneath the Paris Opera House.

After Raoul leaves, the audience hears the booming voice of the elusive Phantom expressing his jealousy over Raoul's visit. Theatergoers and Christine also catch their first glimpse of this masked character. The Phantom appears as a reflection in the mirror in Christine's room but then reaches out to pull Christine through the glass and toward a series of underground tunnels that lead to his lair. The magic of the mirror is one of many famous special effects in the production.

As the two arrive in his hidden chamber, the Phantom sings Christine a romantic lullaby titled "Music of the Night." Entranced, Christine longs to discover what lies behind the mask. When she surprises the Phantom by pulling off the mask, he hurriedly turns from the audience, but Christine spies something that horrifies her. "Can you even dare to look, or bear to think of me?" the Phantom angrily questions her. "This loathsome gargoyle /

Who burns in hell, But secretly yearns for heaven / Secretly, secretly. . . ."[2] Realizing she will be missed at the opera, the Phantom brings her back.

The "Opera Ghost"

As act 1 progresses, audiences learn the Phantom has been sending Firmin, André, Raoul, and Carlotta a series of threatening notes, all signed "O. G." for "Opera Ghost." The Phantom demands Christine be cast as the star in an upcoming production. He urges Raoul to stay away from her as well. Carlotta is outraged by the thought of being replaced, and Firmin and André ultimately decide to keep Carlotta as their leading lady.

The Phantom wreaks revenge by using ventriloquism to make Carlotta croak like a toad in the midst of her performance. Moments later, he hangs a stagehand and drops the body from the rafters. Panic erupts in the theater, and Christine and Raoul flee to the roof, where they profess their love for one another. The Phantom overhears the conversation and is wounded by Christine's betrayal. Back in the theater, as Christine sings Carlotta's role, the Phantom causes the chandelier to crash to the stage floor.

Masks and Masquerades

Act 2 begins with the opera house hosting a colorful masquerade ball. The Phantom has not been heard from in six months, and Raoul and Christine are now secretly engaged. The carnival atmosphere comes to a halt, though, when the opera ghost reappears in a ghoulish costume, complete with a mask in the shape of a skull.

The Phantom tosses Firmin and André the libretto to *Don Juan Triumphant*, an opera he has composed and expects them to stage. He warns Christine that she still belongs to him and then shocks the partygoers by evaporating into thin air. As the second act continues, Raoul asks Madame Giry what she knows of the ghost. She reveals that the Phantom is a brilliant musician cursed by a hideous disfigurement. Armed with the knowledge that the "ghost" is no specter at all, but a violent genius who is controlling his fiancée, Raoul devises a trap.

Raoul asks the managers to stage *Don Juan Triumphant* with Christine in the lead female role, knowing the Phantom will attend and armed guards will be able to capture him at the show. Although

confused about her feelings for her teacher, Christine reluctantly agrees.

But Raoul's strategy backfires. At the opening performance, the Phantom murders the male lead, Piangi, steals his costume, and takes the stage as Don Juan. He and Christine sing a passionate duet, "Past the Point of No Return." When their duet concludes, Christine removes his mask, revealing the Phantom's deformed face to the audience. The Phantom seizes Christine and escapes with her through a trapdoor in the stage floor.

The masquerade ball scene highlights the themes of masks and hidden identities.

The Underground Lair

Thanks to Madame Giry's direction, Raoul is able to pursue the pair to the Phantom's lair just as Piangi's body is discovered and chaos erupts in the opera house. Meanwhile, Christine, who has arrived at the Phantom's underground home, bitterly demands to know what he intends to do with her. As the Phantom laments how his disfigurement has ruined his chances at love, Raoul appears. He almost immediately becomes trapped in a stranglehold, however, as the opera ghost snares him with his magical lasso.

The Phantom orders Christine to make a choice—to either spend the rest of her days with him and thereby save her fiancé or leave and send Raoul to his death. Her decision is revealed when she gently takes the Phantom's unmasked face in her hands and kisses him after praying for the courage to show him a better life than he has known. Amazed and overwhelmed by her display of love, the Phantom releases both Christine and Raoul, ordering them to abandon him and never look back.

As the pair departs, the echoes of a mob seeking revenge for Piangi's death can be heard not far

Sarah Brightman starred as Christine in a 1988 performance of *The Phantom of the Opera* at New York's Majestic Theatre.

from the underground chamber. After the Phantom quietly confesses his undying love for Christine, he swirls his cape around his shoulders and vanishes from the stage. When Madame Giry's daughter, Meg, enters his lair with the angry crowds not far behind her, the only remaining trace she finds of the tragic opera ghost is his white mask. The musical's conclusion, like so much of the overall production, reminds audiences of the power of illusion and concealment—and of man's struggle between wanting to hide and to be seen for who he truly is.

A scene from a 1988 Broadway performance of *The Phantom of the Opera*

How to Apply Psychoanalytic Criticism to *The Phantom of the Opera*

What Is Psychoanalytic Criticism?

Psychoanalytic criticism is the analysis of a work through the lens of psychoanalytic theory. Psychoanalysts Sigmund Freud, Jacques Lacan, and Carl Jung were famous for studying the subconscious behaviors of human beings—hidden impulses and feelings that men and women are usually not even aware of but that affect the way they react to various situations. When analyzing a musical, writers relying on psychoanalytic criticism therefore try to determine what underlying impulses are expressed by the action onstage. Often, they ask whether the work reflects any of the secret, unconscious desires and anxieties of the play's creators.

Critics who evaluate a theater production using this technique must follow a few important steps. First, they need to consider characters' behaviors. They then must psychoanalyze the characters, examining whether the protagonists appear to be motivated by any subconscious feelings. Critics should also examine the plot progression to determine whether it reflects any of the theories of psychological development proposed by Freud, Lacan, or Jung. Critics always need to keep in mind that the object of their psychoanalytic critique is to analyze how subconscious motivations impact the characters and the plot.

Thesis Statement

The thesis statement in this critique is as follows: "Jung's theory of the mask is reflected in Lloyd Webber's *The Phantom of the Opera*, a psychological drama in which the characters are torn between the need to hide various parts of their identities and a longing to reveal their true selves." The thesis answers the following question: How can *Phantom* be understood using psychoanalytic theory?

Critiquing *The Phantom of the Opera*

Swiss psychoanalyst Carl Jung theorized that all human beings adopt a persona, or a "mask," that they wear to impress others and to hide their flaws. At the same time, however, they are motivated by a desire to have the world know them for who they really are. Jung's theory of the mask is reflected in Lloyd Webber's *The Phantom of the Opera*, a psychological drama in which the characters are torn between the need to hide various parts of their identities and a longing to reveal their true selves.

The character of the Phantom is defined by the white mask he wears throughout most of the musical. It makes his presence seem powerful and mysterious to those around him. He is the all-knowing, all-seeing opera ghost who can use magic to disappear through trapdoors and mirrors and who is capable of turning a diva's voice into that of a croaking toad. In reality, though, he is a flesh-and-blood man who sings about how his own mother and society have rejected him because of his disfigured face. He has been wounded and suffers from a great deal of emotional pain.

> **Argument One**
>
> The author offers arguments in support of her thesis statement. Her first point is as follows: "The character of the Phantom is defined by the white mask he wears throughout most of the musical." The author will offer evidence to show the two sides of the Phantom's identity.

In addition, his life is turned upside down by his adoration of Christine Daaé. Part of the Phantom wants Christine to worship him as a father figure and a godlike instructor who always remains somewhat hidden from her by his mask. But he is

Argument Two
The author gives evidence to support her first point. To show the conflicting nature behind the Phantom's mask, she now claims, "Part of the Phantom wants Christine to worship him as a father figure and a godlike instructor who always remains somewhat hidden from her by his mask. But he is eager for Christine to perceive him and love him as a human being as well."

eager for Christine to perceive him and love him as a human being as well. He craves her touch, which is made obvious when he gently takes her hand and places it alongside his face during the song "Music of the Night" in act 1. He is not content to merely hear her beautiful voice onstage; he wants her to be by his side forever and to treat him as a lover—much in the same way as she treats Raoul de Chagny.

The Phantom, however, faces a massive inner struggle. When he wears the mask and remains concealed from the possibly judgmental eyes of Christine and society, he is safe. Everyone will see him as someone who exercises control and authority and who deserves to be feared and respected. He can even manage to win her adoration with his booming yet hypnotic singing voice.

Sadly, though, Christine will never be able to love her teacher as a man who seeks physical affection and emotional reassurance so long as he shields himself by playing the role of the masked

and mysterious opera ghost. If he clings to this identity, she will always keep herself at a distance, both idolizing him from afar and living in terror of him. Much of the Phantom's subconscious turmoil over this dilemma is summed up as he tries to regain her trust after she tears away his mask for the first time in act 1. "Fear can turn to love," he reassures a shocked and frightened Christine, as she cowers in horror a few feet away from him in his underground lair. "You'll learn to see, to find the man behind the monster / This repulsive carcass / Who seems a beast but secretly dreams of beauty / Secretly, secretly. . . ."[1]

The theme of hidden identities runs throughout the plotline of *The Phantom of the Opera*.

Jung's concept of masks and illusions is represented in other elements of the production as well. The musical illustrates this subconscious tension between hidden and revealed identities during the visually stunning number "Masquerade," which is performed at the beginning of act 2. As the opera house hosts a colorful masquerade ball, Christine is at first delighted by the swirling costumes and masks that surround her. Ironically, she is trying to hide an engagement necklace she has received from Raoul because she fears the Phantom will become violently jealous if he learns of their relationship. The lyrics of the song "Masquerade" reflect her efforts: "Hide your face, so the world will never find you!"[2]

The masks allow the characters to temporarily forget their worries and insecurities and appear however they want society to see them. As the party continues, though, Christine begins to find that the costumes and concealment stir unpleasant emotions within her. As she is whisked from one dancer to

---

Argument Three

The author is now discussing characters other than the Phantom. She states, "The musical illustrates this subconscious tension between hidden and revealed identities during the visually stunning number 'Masquerade,' which is performed at the beginning of act 2."

another during a waltz, she cannot help but wonder whether the mask she is staring up at belongs to the Phantom himself. As terrifying as reality can be, she discovers that a world in which people hide from reality can be equally unsettling.

Emmy Rossum, *right*, and Gerard Butler, *left*, in the film version of *The Phantom of the Opera*

Conclusion

This final paragraph is the conclusion of the critique. The author invites the reader to compare the physical world with the world of illusion in which the Phantom appeared to live. In the end, the world of illusion was itself a false image, as the Phantom's mask proves that he was indeed a living man.

After the Phantom proves to the audience one last time that he is a master of illusion by vanishing into thin air, one of the few traces that remains of him is his haunting white mask. The audience is reminded once again that the mask was a tool to hide the Phantom's real identity. Ironically, as the curtain falls, the most convincing evidence that Lloyd Webber's title character was a flesh-and-blood man—and not the phantom that he used the mask to portray himself to be—is the mask itself.

Thinking Critically about *The Phantom of the Opera*

Now it's your turn to assess the critique.
Consider these questions:

1. The author's thesis addresses Jung's theory of masks and identity. Can you think of additional details from *Phantom* that also might back up the thesis?

2. Are there any other approaches someone applying a psychoanalytic criticism to this work might take? What additional questions could a critic evaluating *Phantom* with this theory develop?

3. Do you agree with the thesis now that you have read all the evidence supporting it? If your answer is no, explain why. Can you identify points you could use to refute the author's argument?

Other Approaches

What you have just read is one way to apply psychoanalytic criticism to *The Phantom of the Opera*. What are some other ways to do so? Sigmund Freud, Jacques Lacan, Carl Jung, and other psychoanalysts have put forth many theories that can be applied to the musical. Following are two alternate approaches.

The Phantom's Humanity

Elements of illusion are a large part of the allure of *The Phantom of the Opera*. Trapdoors, mirrors, and magical disappearances contribute to the haunting spectacle. But in the end, the Phantom leaves behind his mask, reminding the audience that he is no ghost, but a flesh-and-blood human who is capable of feeling pain. Jungian analyst Bernice Hill provides commentary on the humanity of the Phantom: "We cannot become human without being first 'seen' and cared for by another."[3]

A thesis statement for a related essay might be: Although the Phantom wishes to hide away from the world that has rejected him, his affection for Christine drives him to forsake his phantom identity, revealing that he is no ghost, but a feeling human being.

Phantom and Archetype Theory

Some critics have analyzed *The Phantom of the Opera* with reference to psychoanalyst Carl Jung's concept of archetypes. Jung defined an archetype as a well-known character type, plotline, or image that recurs throughout myth and literature, such as the caring mother, the fearless hero on a quest, the courageous underdog, or the bitter outcast. Jung theorized that archetypes were stored in the "collective unconscious" of all human beings, which explains why they are so universally understood.

A thesis statement for an essay that discusses archetypes in *The Phantom of the Opera* might read as follows: The audience ultimately sympathizes with the Phantom, who is portrayed as the archetypal outcast—a person rejected by society who becomes bitter and twisted in response.

You Critique It

Now that you have learned about several different critical theories and how to apply them to musical theater productions, are you ready to perform a critique of your own? You have read that this type of evaluation can help you look at musicals from a new perspective and make you pay attention to certain issues you may not have otherwise recognized. So, why not use one of the critical theories profiled in this book to consider a fresh take on your favorite musical?

First, choose a theory and the musical you want to analyze. Remember that the theory is a springboard for asking questions about the work.

Next, write a specific question that relates to the theory you have selected. Then you can form your thesis, which should provide the answer to that question. Your thesis is the most important part of your critique and offers an argument about the work based on the tenets, or beliefs, of the theory you are applying. Recall that the thesis statement typically appears at the very end of the introductory paragraph of your essay. It is usually only one sentence long.

After you have written your thesis, find evidence to back it up. Good places to start are in the work itself or journals or articles that discuss what other people have said about it. You may also want to read about the composer's life so you can get a sense of what factors may have affected the creative process. This can be especially useful if working within historical, biographical, or psychological criticism.

Depending on which theory you are applying, you can often find evidence in the musical's scenery, lyrics, plots, or musical styles. You also should explore parts of the musical that seem to disprove your thesis and create an argument against them. As you do this, you might want to address what other critics have written about the musical. Their quotes may help support your claim.

Before you start analyzing a work, think about the different arguments made in this book. Reflect on how evidence supporting the thesis was presented. Did you find that some of the techniques used to back up the arguments were more convincing than others? Try these methods as you prove your thesis in your own critique.

When you are finished writing your critique, read it over carefully. Is your thesis statement understandable? Do the supporting arguments flow logically, with the topic of each paragraph clearly stated? Can you add any information that would present your readers with a stronger argument in favor of your thesis? Were you able to use lyrics from the musical to enhance your ideas?

Did you see the work in a new light?

Timeline

1948 Andrew Lloyd Webber is born in London, England, on March 22.

1965 Lloyd Webber completes high school at London's Westminster School.

He begins studying history at Oxford University's Magdalen College but drops out after one term to concentrate on composing.

1983 Lloyd Webber and Hugill divorce.

1984 *Starlight Express* premieres.

Lloyd Webber marries second wife Sarah Brightman.

1986 *The Phantom of the Opera* debuts at Her Majesty's Theatre in London on October 9.

1990 Lloyd Webber and Brightman divorce.

1991 Lloyd Webber weds third wife, Madeleine Astrid Gurdon.

1992 Lloyd Webber is knighted by Queen Elizabeth II; she names him a British lord five years later.

1997 "You Must Love Me" from the film *Evita* is awarded a Golden Globe for Best Original Song. It is later awarded an Academy Award for Best Original Song.

1967 — Lloyd Webber enrolls as a student of musical theater at the Royal College of Music in London.

1968 — *Joseph and the Amazing Technicolor Dreamcoat* premieres on March 1 at a boys' preparatory school in London.

1971 — *Jesus Christ Superstar* debuts on October 12, 1971, at the Mark Hellinger Theatre on Broadway in New York.

Lloyd Webber marries Sarah Tudor Hugill.

1978 — *Evita* premieres at the Prince Edward Theatre in London on June 21.

1981 — *Cats* debuts at the New London Theatre in London on May 11.

1982 — The full-length version of *Joseph* opens at the Royale Theatre on Broadway; *Song and Dance* debuts as well.

2004 — Director Joel Schumacher releases a film version of *Phantom*.

2006 — *The Sound of Music* reopens in London, with Lloyd Webber acting as producer of the latest version of the classic stage production by Rodgers and Hammerstein.

2009 — In October, Lloyd Webber reveals to the public that he is suffering from prostate cancer. After an operation, he is found to be cancer-free.

2010 — *Love Never Dies*, the sequel to *Phantom*, premieres in March.

Glossary

archetype
>   Any character, plot, or image that recurs through the myths and literature of all cultures and historical periods.

ballad
>   A short, slow song, typically with a romantic or sentimental theme.

Broadway
>   A street in Manhattan, New York, that is famous for its theaters.

choreography
>   The arrangement of dancing for the stage.

collaborate
>   To work together on a project.

Grammys
>   The Grammys, or Grammy Awards, are awards presented annually by the National Academy of Recording Arts and Sciences to acknowledge outstanding achievements in the music industry.

ironically
>   In a manner that is completely opposite to what may have been expected or anticipated.

libretto
>   The text of a musical production.

lyricist
>   A person who writes the words to a song.

pop
> Popular music, especially that which appeals to teenagers. Pop is generally a lighter version of rock and roll with strong rhythm and harmony and emphasis on romantic love.

protagonist
> The main character in a play or other literary work.

psychoanalysts
> Professionals who study people's underlying motives and sometimes use their observations to help rid their patients of mental or emotional disorders.

rock opera
> A production that is sung like a traditional opera but features rock and roll instead of classical music in some or all of its score.

sacrilegious
> Disrespectful of sacred beliefs or traditions.

score
> The sheet music for a musical composition, written in musical notation.

subconscious
> Impulses or emotions that people are often not even aware they are experiencing but that frequently affect their responses to various situations.

Tonys
> The Tonys, or Tony Awards, are awards presented annually by the American Theatre Wing and the Broadway League to acknowledge outstanding achievements in live American theater.

Bibliography of Works and Criticism

Important Works

Music composed by Lloyd Webber except where otherwise noted.

The Likes of Us, 1966

Joseph and the Amazing Technicolor Dreamcoat, 1968

Jesus Christ Superstar, 1971

Evita, 1978

Tell Me on a Sunday, 1979

Cats, 1981

Song and Dance, 1982

Starlight Express, 1984

The Phantom of the Opera, 1986

Aspects of Love, 1989

Sunset Boulevard, 1993

By Jeeves, 1996 (originally released as *Jeeves* in 1975)

Whistle Down the Wind, 1996

The Beautiful Game, 2000

Bombay Dreams, 2002 (as producer; music by A. R. Rahman)

The Woman in White, 2004

Sound of Music, 2006 (as producer; music and lyrics by Rodgers
    and Hammerstein)

Love Never Dies, 2010

Critical Discussions

Carlson, Marvin Albert. *Performance: A Critical Introduction*. New York: Routledge, 2004.

Critical Theory and Performance. Ed. Janelle G. Reinelt and Joseph R. Roach. Ann Arbor, MI: University of Michigan Press, 2007.

Resources

Selected Bibliography

Citron, Stephen. *Sondheim and Lloyd-Webber: The New Musical*. New York: Oxford University Press, 2001.

Lloyd Webber, Andrew. *Cats: The Book of the Musical*. San Diego: Harcourt Brace Jovanovich, 1983.

Perry, George. *The Complete* Phantom of the Opera. New York: H. Holt, 1998.

Snelson, John. *Andrew Lloyd Webber*. New Haven, CT: Yale University Press, 2004.

Further Readings

Belli, Mary Lou. *Acting for Young Actors: The Ultimate Teen Guide*. New York: Back Stage Books, 2006.

Lerch, Louis, comp. *Musical Theatre Anthology for Teens: Duets Edition*. Winona, MN: Hal Leonard, 2001.

Ryan, Michael. *Literary Theory: A Practical Introduction*. 2nd ed. Malden, MA: Blackwell Publishing, 2007.

Web Links

To learn more about critiquing the works of Andrew Lloyd Webber, visit ABDO Publishing Company online at **www.abdopublishing.com**. Web sites about the works of Andrew Lloyd Webber are featured on our Book Links page. These links are routinely monitored and updated to provide the most current information available.

For More Information

Andrew Lloyd Webber

c/o The Really Useful Group

22 Tower Street, London, WC2H 9TW

www.andrewlloydwebber.com

This site features news and updates about Andrew Lloyd Webber and his productions.

The Theatre Museum

40 Worth Street, Suite 824, New York, NY 10013

212-764-4112 x 201

www.thetheatremuseum.org

Exhibitions and events at this site promote knowledge about the history and current productions in theater.

Source Notes

Chapter 1. Introduction to Critiques

None.

Chapter 2. A Closer Look at Andrew Lloyd Webber

None.

Chapter 3. An Overview of *Jesus Christ Superstar*

1. Tim Rice and Andrew Lloyd Webber. *Jesus Christ Superstar: A Rock Opera: Musical Excerpts, Complete Libretto*. London: Leeds Music, 1970. 51.

Chapter 4. How to Apply Historical Criticism to *Jesus Christ Superstar*

1. Tim Rice and Andrew Lloyd Webber. *Jesus Christ Superstar: A Rock Opera: Musical Excerpts, Complete Libretto*. London: Leeds Music, 1970. 45.

2. Ibid.

3. Ibid. 58.

4. Michael Walsh. *Andrew Lloyd Webber: His Life and Works*. New York: Harry N. Abrams, 1989. 77.

5. Martin Brady. "Boiler Room brings the ultimate hippie passion play back to life in *Jesus Christ Superstar*." *Nashville Scene*. 27 Aug. 2009. 12 Apr. 2010 < http://www.nashvillescene.com/nashvilleboiler-room-brings-the-ultimate-hippie-passionplay-back-to-life-in-jesus-christ-superstar/Content?oid=1202387>.

Chapter 5. An Overview of *Evita*

1. Tim Rice and Andrew Lloyd Webber. *Evita: Musical Excerpts and Complete Libretto*. Melville, NY: Leeds Music Corp, 1979. 57.

2. Ibid. 70.

Chapter 6. How to Apply Feminist Criticism to *Evita*

1. Tim Rice and Andrew Lloyd Webber. *Evita: Musical Excerpts and Complete Libretto*. Melville, NY: Leeds Music Corp, 1979. 9.

2. Ibid. 64.

3. Ibid. 47.

4. Ibid. 62.

5. Marta E. Savigliano. "Evita: The Globalization of a National Myth." *Ohio-State.edu*. Nov. 1997. 11 Oct. 2009 <http://people.cohumsohio-state.edu/guy60/history534.04/Savigliano.pdf>.

6. John Berger. "Dynamic Women Bring Emotion to ACT's *Evita*." *Honolulu Star-Bulletin Online*. 17 May 2001. 11 Oct. 2009 <http://www.armytheatre.com evitarev.html>.

Source Notes Continued

Chapter 7. An Overview of *Cats*

1. Andrew Lloyd Webber. *Vocal Selections from Cats*. Milwaukee, WI: H. Leonard, 1981. 102.

Chapter 8. How to Apply New Criticism to *Cats*

1. Andrew Lloyd Webber. *Vocal Selections from Cats*. Milwaukee, WI: H. Leonard, 1981. 106.

2. Ibid. 18.

3. Stephen Holden. "Theater on Video; More Intimate 'Cats.'" *New York Times Online*. 1 Nov. 1998. 7 Feb. 2010 <http://www.nytimes.com/1998/11/01/theater/theater-on-video-more-intimate-cats.html?pagewanted=1>.

4. Michael Walsh. *Andrew Lloyd Webber: His Life and Works*. New York: Harry N. Abrams, 1989. 127.

Chapter 9. An Overview of *The Phantom of the Opera*

1. George Perry. *The Complete* Phantom of the Opera. New York: H. Holt, 1998. 145.

2. Ibid. 147.

Chapter 10. How to Apply Psychoanalytic Criticism to *The Phantom of the Opera*

1. George Perry. *The Complete* Phantom of the Opera. New York: H. Holt, 1998. 144.

2. Ibid. 155.

3. Bernice H. Hill. "Reflections on *The Phantom of the Opera*." *The Jung Page*. 22 Dec. 2005. 3 Nov. 2009 <http://www.cgjungpage.org/index.php?option=com_content&task=view&id=741&Itemid=40>.

Index

About the Author

Katie Marsico is the author of more than 50 books for children and young adults. She lives with her husband, daughter, and two sons in Elmhurst, Illinois. Katie worked as a managing editor in children's publishing before becoming a full-time writer.

Photo Credits

Pool, Christian Charisius/AP Images, cover, 1; iStockphoto, cover; Birgitte Magnus/iStockphoto, cover; Yarek Gnatowski/iStockphoto, cover; File/AP Images, 12; Evening Standard/Getty Images, 15; Gabriela Maj/Getty Images, 19; Dave Caulkin/AP Images, 20; Jens Meyer/AP Images, 25; John Olson/Getty Images, 26; Edgar R.Schoepal/AP Images, 31, 99; AP Images, 33; Photofest, 38, 43, 51, 74; Alastair Grant/AP Images, 41, 46, 53; Buena Vista Pictures/Photofest, 45; Keystone, Alessandro della Valle/AP Images, 58, 67, 68; Richard Drew/AP Images, 63; Nigel Teare/AP Images, 64, 98 (top); Warner Bros./Photofest, 77, 81, 89, 91; Ed Bailey/AP Images, 83, 98 (bottom); Joan Marcus/Photofest, 84